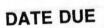

DATE DUE

PRINTED IN U.S.A.

BATMAN
AND
ROBIN

VOLUM ... AMIAN

WITHDRAWN

BATMAN AND ROBIN

VOLUME 4
REQUIEM FOR DAMIAN

PETER J. **TOMASI** writer

PATRICK **GLEASON**
CLIFF **RICHARDS** pencillers

MICK **GRAY**   MARK **IRWIN**
MARLO **ALQUIZA** inkers

JOHN **KALISZ** colorist

TAYLOR **ESPOSITO**
CARLOS M. **MANGUAL** letterers

PATRICK **GLEASON**, MICK **GRAY** & JOHN **KALISZ**
collection and original cover artists

BATMAN created by BOB **KANE**

RACHEL GLUCKSTERN Editor – Original Series RICKEY PURDIN DARREN SHAN Assistant Editors – Original Series
RACHEL PINNELAS Editor ROBBIN BROSTERMAN Design Director – Books ROBBIE BIEDERMAN Publication Design

BOB HARRAS Senior VP – Editor-in-Chief, DC Comics

DIANE NELSON President DAN DIDIO and JIM LEE Co-Publishers GEOFF JOHNS Chief Creative Officer
AMIT DESAI Senior VP – Marketing and Franchise Management
AMY GENKINS Senior VP – Business and Legal Affairs NAIRI GARDINER Senior VP – Finance
JEFF BOISON VP – Publishing Planning MARK CHIARELLO VP – Art Direction and Design
JOHN CUNNINGHAM VP – Marketing TERRI CUNNINGHAM VP – Editorial Administration
LARRY GANEM VP – Talent Relations and Services ALISON GILL Senior VP – Manufacturing and Operations
HANK KANALZ Senior VP – Vertigo and Integrated Publishing JAY KOGAN VP – Business and Legal Affairs, Publishing
JACK MAHAN VP – Business Affairs, Talent NICK NAPOLITANO VP – Manufacturing Administration SUE POHJA VP – Book Sales
FRED RUIZ VP – Manufacturing Operations COURTNEY SIMMONS Senior VP – Publicity BOB WAYNE Senior VP – Sales

BATMAN AND ROBIN VOLUME 4: REQUIEM FOR DAMIAN

DC Comics, 1700 Broadway, New York, NY 10019
A Warner Bros. Entertainment Company.
Printed by RR Donnelley, Owensville, MO, USA. 10/24/14. First Printing.
ISBN: 978-1-4012-5058-4

Library of Congress Cataloging-in-Publication Data

Tomasi, Peter, author.
Batman and Robin. Vol. 4, Requiem for Damian / Peter Tomasi ; illustrated by Patrick Gleason ; illustrated by Mick Gray.
pages cm. — (The New 52!)
ISBN 978-1-4012-5058-4
1. Graphic novels. I. Gleason, Patrick, illustrator. II. Gray, Mick, illustrator. III. Title. IV. Title: Requiem for Damian.
PN6728.B36T646 2014
741.5'973—dc23
                    2014008595

*FROM *CYMBELINE*
BY WILLIAM SHAKESPEARE

YOU LEFT THESE BACK AT OUR DOOR.

I DIDN'T LEAVE THEM FOR YOU, MISTER WAYNE, I LEFT THEM FOR *HIM.*

--OUT OF THE WAY-- LOOK OUT--

MASTER BRUCE, IS THERE SOMETHING--

WHERE'S DAMIAN?!

--WRONG?

GET US OUT OF HERE, ALFRED.

NOW.

KSSSS

BATMAN OF GOTHAM.
I HAVE HEARD QUITE A
BIT ABOUT YOU OVER
THE YEARS.

GLAD
TO HEAR
IT.

YOU'RE
A HARD
MONSTER TO
GET IN TOUCH
WITH.

THIS IS NOT HOW--OR
WHERE--I ENVISIONED
OUR FIRST MEETING
TAKING PLACE.

HOW DID
YOU FIND CASTLE
FRANKENSTEIN?

THE SUPER-HUMAN ADVANCED
DEFENSE EXECUTIVE'S FILES
AREN'T AS SECURE AS
FATHER TIME THINKS.

I AM QUITE
SURE MY FELLOW
AGENTS ARE ON THE
WAY HERE EVEN AS
WE SPEAK.

I DOUBT
IT.

HRRM.

I TOOK
THE LIBERTY
OF REMOVING
AND DISABLING THE
S.H.A.D.E. NET IMPLANT
FROM THE BACK OF
YOUR NECK BEFORE
WE ARRIVED
HERE.

WHAT MANNER OF
SUBSTANCE ARE YOU
RESTRAINING ME
WITH?

JUSTICE
LEAGUE PROTOTYPE--
CLASSIFIED. DIDN'T THINK
YOU'D COME OF YOUR
OWN VOLITION.

A CORRECT
ASSUMPTION...AND BY
THE RENEWED APPEARANCE
OF MY CREATOR'S
ANCIENT LAB...

KRRKKR

KKRRK

...I TAKE IT
YOU HAVE BEEN
SEARCHING FOR
SOMETHING.

YES.

HOW DID THE KID COME AND GO-- WHO BROUGHT HIM TO THE CAMPUS THEATER?

THERE WAS ALWAYS A LIMO PARKED OUT BACK-- BLACK WINDOWS-- NEVER SAW INSIDE-- FIGURED IF IT WASN'T HIS FATHER IT WAS A STAFF CHAUFFEUR.

COME TO THINK OF IT, I NEVER SAW HIM ACTUALLY GET INTO IT.

WELL, IT'S NOT LIKE A TEN-YEAR-OLD KNOWS HOW TO DRIVE--ESPECIALLY A BIG CAR LIKE THAT, RIGHT?

...UM, YEAH, RIGHT.

GUESS YOU'LL NEED TO FIND ANOTHER STUDENT.

WHAT I REALLY WANT TO DO IS DIRECT

HOPE NOT. MAYBE HE'LL BE BACK. DAMIAN WAS A REAL NATURAL. I KINDA MISS HIM.

AND THE MONTHLY RENT NUT, YOU'RE THE ONLY ROOMIE WHO EVER PAYS ON TIME.

SHOULDN'T BE A PROBLEM. MISTER WAYNE SETTLED UP.

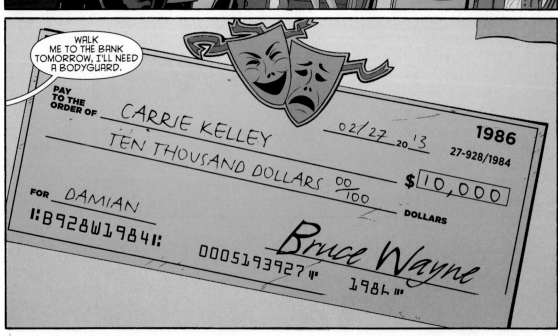

WALK ME TO THE BANK TOMORROW, I'LL NEED A BODYGUARD.

PAY TO THE ORDER OF ___CARRIE KELLEY___   02/27 20 13   **1986**
                                                           27-928/1984

___TEN THOUSAND DOLLARS___ 00/100 _____ $ 10,000

_____ DOLLARS

FOR ___DAMIAN___

⑈B928W1984⑈   0005193927⑈   1986⑈   *Bruce Wayne*

BATMAN AND THE RED HOOD: RAGE

PATRICK GLEASON & CLIFF RICHARDS pencillers **MICK GRAY & MARK JOHN IRWIN** inkers

I SEE YOU'RE *WORKING* TO KEEP YOUR CARBON FOOTPRINT SMALL.

CAN I ASK YOU SOME-THING?

SURE, WHAT?

WHY WAS *DAMIAN* TAKING *ACTING* LESSONS?

HE SAID HE WANTED TO SEE WHAT IT WAS LIKE BEING *SOMEONE ELSE.*

IS THAT RIGHT?

YEP.

NICE-LOOKING FAMILY.

WOW, *HOBSON'S* BEEN HERE FOREVER-- LOOK HOW *YOUNG* HE IS IN THIS ONE.

THIS MONEY I GAVE YOU IS FOR LESSONS OWED ALONG WITH COMPENSATING YOU FOR NOT GIVING NOTICE.

I PULLED OUT THE THOUSAND I EARNED--THE REST IS YOURS--I DON'T TAKE MONEY FOR WORK I HAVEN'T DONE, MISTER WAYNE.

RRFF

TITUS USUALLY **DOESN'T** TAKE TO STRANGERS VERY WELL.

"I HAVE DOGS, MY LORD, WILL ROUSE THE PROUDEST PANTHER IN THE CHASE, AND CLIMB THE HIGHEST PROMONTORY TOP."

RRRM

GREAT DANES WERE BRED TO HUNT WILD BOAR IN GERMANY OVER A THOUSAND YEARS AGO. A NICE COMBO OF AN IRISH WOLFHOUND AND ENGLISH MASTIFF.

THEY'RE REFERRED TO SOMETIMES AS THE "APOLLO" OF DOGS.

YOU SEEM TO KNOW QUITE A BIT ABOUT OUR **LITTLE PUP**, MS. KELLEY.

MY MOTHER OWNED A KENNEL FOR A FEW YEARS WHEN I WAS A KID. TITUS COULD USE SOME MORE EXERCISE, BUT NOT TOO STRENUOUS BECAUSE THEY'RE PRONE TO ARTHRITIS AND HIP DYSPLASIA.

RRRF

ALFRED CAN HANDLE TITUS AND ALSO SHOW YOU TO THE **DOOR.**

POOR OL' *HOBSON* HERE'S AGING PRETTY DAMN QUICK--BET YOU'RE STRESSING HIM OUT WITH ALL THIS WORK.

GOOD DAY, MISS KELLEY.

"AND I HAVE HORSE WILL FOLLOW WHERE THE GAME MAKES WAY, AND RUNS LIKE SWALLOWS O'ER THE PLAIN."

A FAN OF SHAKESPEARE'S 'TITUS ANDRONICUS,' HMM?

YEP, THAT OLD MOVIE WITH ANTHONY HOPKINS AND JESSICA LANGE IS GREAT.

THE FILM IS NOT *THAT* OLD.

ACTUALLY, IT KINDA *IS.*

BY THE WAY, WHO NAMED HIM TITUS?

DAMIAN.

WOULD YOU LIKE A JOB TAKING CARE OF TITUS HERE AT THE HOUSE TWO OR THREE TIMES A WEEK, GAS AND FOOD INCLUDED?

ABSOLUTELY, I'D LOVE TO WATCH HIM TILL DAMIAN GETS BACK, BUT WHAT ABOUT *MISTER GRUMPY* IN THERE?

NO WORRIES.

HIS *BARK* IS WORSE THAN HIS *BITE.*

WHAT AM I LOOKING AT?

A CADRE OF *INTERNATIONAL BOUNTY HUNTERS*-- ALL SNIPERS--EXPERT MARKSMEN AND WOMEN WHO TRAVEL THE GLOBE LOOKING FOR BIG PAYDAYS FROM INDIVIDUALS AND COUNTRIES ALIKE.

THEY OPERATE LIKE A SMALL COMPANY, *DONATING* A PERCENTAGE OF THEIR BOUNTIES INTO A FUND TO PROCURE HI-TECH SURVEILLANCE AND WEAPONS SO THEY'RE *ALWAYS* AHEAD OF THE CURVE AGAINST HIGH *RISK* AND HIGH *VALUE* ASSETS.

THEY'RE BASED IN *ETHIOPIA*, PROTECTED BY POLITICIANS IN THE *STATE GOVERNMENT* WHO *AVERT* THEIR EYES AS LONG AS REGULAR DEPOSITS ARE MADE INTO THEIR *OFFSHORE ACCOUNTS*, AND THE OPPOSITION PARTY IS CULLED FROM TIME TO TIME BY A WELL-AIMED NIGHT SCOPE IN SECRET STATE-SANCTIONED FREEBIES.

SOME OF THESE *SHOOTERS* CAME HUNTING FOR DAMIAN WHEN *TALIA* PLACED A *HALF BILLION-DOLLAR BOUNTY* ON HIM.

I THINK IT'S TIME TO SHOW THESE BASTARDS THAT TARGETING A *TEN-YEAR-OLD* PUTS A BULL'S-EYE ON THEMSELVES...

...AND THAT KILLING ISN'T MUCH OF A LIVING.

YOU ASKING ME TO GO WITH YOU?

YES, I AM.

WHY?

BECAUSE I'M SEEING *RED*.

Everything.

The Joker.

The cave.

The broken trust.

Damian.

Tell him.

Tell him
y you're
not...

Maybe he'll

Best part of my **job's** the quiet. The sounds of silence.

Splendid isolation, one to answer to.

Just me being me and getting the thing that needs getting...

...which tonight is something called the "Ram in a Thicket," a golden figurine that dates back to 2400 B.C.

Got its name from a guy named Woolley who exca[va]ted it from the Royal Cemete[ry] at Ur in Southern Iraq ba[ck] in 1928.

My client's 4-1-1 sai[d] called it that becaus[e] reminded him of the [story of] Abraham all set to k[ill his] son, Isaac, in the Bo[ok of] Genesis until he was [saved] by a ram tangled in [the] bushes.

Sure was Isaac's lucky day.

And mine too, since this'll be a nice payout if I keep Penguin from getting a peck of the action.

INCOMING JLA TRANSMISSION.

WHAT'S *SHE* DOING HERE?

MS. KELLEY GIVES HER *UNDIVIDED* ATTENTION TO *TITUS* THREE TIMES A WEEK.

DON'T *YOU* DO THAT?

UNDIVIDED IS THE OPERATIVE WORD, SIR.

YOU'RE IN COLLEGE. DON'T YOU HAVE CLASS?

IT'S *SUNDAY.*

DON'T YOU HAVE *ANYTHING* BETTER TO DO?

WHAT'S *BETTER* THAN MAKING A MOVIE ABOUT A DOG? "A DAY IN THE LIFE OF TITUS." A LOT EASIER THAN DAMIAN TRYING TO *SKYPE* WITH HIM FROM SIX TIME ZONES AWAY.

YOU AND DAMIAN MADE A STRONG CONNECTION PRETTY QUICKLY FOR ONCE-A-WEEK SESSIONS.

WE DID, HE FEELS LIKE THE LITTLE BROTHER I NEVER HAD-- TOUGH ON THE OUTSIDE, MARSHMALLOW ON THE INSIDE.

AND HIS HONESTY AND LACK OF... WELL...CRAP...IS REFRESHING COMPARED TO MY OTHER STUDENTS AND FELLOW DRAMA CLASSMATES WHO ALL THINK THEY'VE WON BEST ACTING *OSCARS* ALREADY.

YES...DAMIAN IS USUALLY ONE FOR SPEAKING HIS MIND...

...A VERY... *INDEPENDENT*- MINDED YOUNG BOY.

WHO, BY THE WAY, STILL *HASN'T* CALLED ME.

--ONE'S THE MOVIE I MADE OF TITUS LAST WEEK AND THE OTHER DRIVE IS THE INTERVIEW--AND YOU, MISTER WAYNE, SEND THE MOVIE TO DAMIAN AND MAKE SURE HE CALLS ME BEFORE THE WEEK IS OUT.

PERSISTENT.

ALWAYS. DO WE HAVE A DEAL?

YES.

WELL, OKAY THEN. HERE.

NOT STAYING FOR LUNCH, MS. KELLEY?

GOT A TWO O' CLOCK MATINEE.

ARE YOU PERFORMING IN A PLAY?

NO, I'M AN USHER AT THE BARRYMORE ON WEEKENDS--I GET TO EARN A FEW EXTRA BUCKS AND SEE A SHOW.

SEIZE THE DAY, MS. KELLEY, SEIZE THE DAY.

RRFF RRFF

TITUS DOES LIKE HAVING SOME YOUTHFUL EXUBERANCE AROUND THE HOUSE.

DIDN'T WE ALL.

RRR

ROBIN COM-LINK TRACK 1 IDENTIFIED.

DIGITAL AUDIO SPLICING SELECTED.

ROBIN COM-LINK TRACK 2 IDENTIFIED.

DIGITAL AUDIO SPLICING SELECTED.

RRFF RRFF

ROBIN COM-LINK TRACK 3 IDENTIFIED.

DIGITAL AUDIO SPLICING SELECTED.

ROBIN COM-LINK TRACK 4 IDENTIFIED.

DIGITAL AUDIO SPLICING SELECTED.

HELLO, SON.

YOUR FRIEND, CARRIE, ASKED ME TO GIVE THIS TO YOU.

CONNECTING CALL TO CARRIE KELLEY— 546-555-1212

DAMIAN AUDIO FILE   UPLOADING   CARRIE KELLEY

Rrrr

B-DEEP
B-DEEP
B-DEEP

AH, HOME
SWEET--

--HOME?

MEOW.

After punching in your other one a few
days ago, figured it was the least I could
do.
Took the liberty of making it a little less
scary for when you're playing JLA with
your new friends.

DON'T MIND ME.

--WE WON'T--

--MESSAGE ON THE MACHINE--

BLEEP!

HI, CARRIE, IT'S DAMIAN.

GOT THE "DAY IN THE LIFE OF TITUS" DVD IN AN OVERNIGHT COURIER POUCH FROM MY FATHER. THANKS, IT WAS GREAT TO SEE EVERYBODY.

MY FATHER MENTIONED YOU'D BE WORKING FOR ALFRED TO HELP CARE FOR TITUS-- I'M GLAD--IT'S GOOD FOR TITUS AND IT HELPS YOU FINANCIALLY.

I APOLOGIZE FOR NOT TELLING YOU ABOUT LEAVING.

I REALLY MISS OUR SESSIONS, BUT MY FATHER SENT ME TO BEIJING FOR THE NEXT FEW MONTHS TO BROADEN MY HORIZONS AND WORK ON MY MANDARIN, FOLLOWED BY SOME STOPS IN JAPAN AND NEW ZEALAND.

I PROMISE TO TAKE IN SOME LIVE THEATER WHILE I'M HERE.

WITH THE MAJOR TIME ZONE DIFFERENCE, LET'S KEEP IN TOUCH BY EMAIL.

TAKE CARE AND GOOD LUCK IN YOUR SOPHOMORE YEAR.

Hmm, AROUND THE WORLD WITH DAMIAN WAYNE.

PLING

NO.

NNGG

DURING EACH OF THOSE FUTILE SECONDS AS YOU STRUGGLE TO *FREE* YOURSELF...

...KNOW THAT I'VE *BEATEN* YOU AT YOUR OWN STUPID, CHILDISH GAME OF CLUES AND TRAPS, MASKS AND TOYS.

RRGHH

KNOW THAT BY THE TIME YOU GET *FREE*, ALL OF IT WILL BE GONE.

YOUR SON. YOUR FAMILY AND FRIENDS.

YOUR PRECIOUS CITY.

GONE.

GLRRGG

GONE BECAUSE THE BATMAN WAS TOO LATE.

TOO LATE TO SAVE THEM.

TOO LATE TO SAVE EVEN HIMSELF.

RESET SIMULATION.

ALFRED PENNYWORTH RECOGNIZED. INTERNET 3.0 RESURRECTION PROGRAM 449 INITIALIZED.

PLEASE BEGIN.

WHAT IS IT, MASTER DAMIAN?

THIS IS IT, PENNYWORTH. FATHER'S ABOUT TO FACE MY MOTHER'S CONTEMPT ON AN EPIC SCALE.

I *ALSO* WANT YOU TO KNOW...

...HOW VERY PROUD *I AM* OF YOU, DAMIAN.

I'LL NEVER FORGIVE MYSELF FOR LETTING YOU LEAVE THE CAVE THAT NIGHT.

PAGE 1

And away we go for our full silent issue, Patrick. Aside from the splash image they subbed for the cover, Batman should appear even more sinister and foreboding during this issue in his body language and demeanor.

Also important is to give a sense of emptiness by the way you frame Batman/Bruce and Alfred during the course of the book. Negative space around their bodies/figures is key to get a sense of the isolation.

Pat, we're at Wayne Manor, specifically in Damian's room. This opening takes place at sunset as Bruce is sitting in a chair in front of the fireplace across from Damian's empty bed simply staring at it as the sun sinks outside, casting a shadow slowly across Bruce's features as the page progresses. This is a real character showcase, so go crazy on the facial details, which you draw so amazingly.

Panel 1

Angle close only on Bruce's eyes, as they look at us. There should be a sense of weariness and pain, yet a cold fury behind them too if you can pull it off.

Panel 2

Pull back a bit so we see more of Bruce's face and the shadow of the night moving across it.

Panel 3

Pull back some more so we see his head and shoulders, his gaze still fixed off panel.

PAGE 2

Splash.

We finally get to see a version of that cool foreboding shot of Bruce sitting in the high-back chair with Titus beside him in front of the smaller fireplace in Damian's room rather than the main one which you first envisioned. Anyway, there's no Damian, of course, and no painting above the mantle.

What Bruce is focused on is Damian's bed in the foreground. We can still see the indentation on his pillow.

TITLE AND CREDITS

PAGE 3
Panel 1
Angle on Bruce as he's gotten up from the chair and walks towards Damian's desk.
Titus follows. And this could be a good spot to set the time of day and why the shadows were crossing his face by showing the window and the sun setting outside with the rays cutting lower through the room.

Panel 2
Angle over Bruce's shoulder as he's got a medium-sized sketchbook of Damian's opened on the desk in front of him. Also indicate a sheet of paper poking out from in-between some pages that he'll see in a moment. The pencil sketches should be of Titus, Alfred, and Damian's new cat too from BATMAN INC, and of course, Bruce, and maybe some other interesting sketches you feel would work, Pat. Maybe a sketch of some fireflies over the Wayne graves. This is obviously different from the violent images we saw earlier in the series to show some growth.

Panel 3
Angle looking up at Bruce looking through the sketchbook. Remember to keep the paper sheet poking out as he gets closer to it. Emotion is visible on his face.

Panel 4
Another shot of Bruce's perspective of the sketchbook. You choose what images, Pat. Ditto on the paper sheet.

Panel 5
Angle on Bruce as he's turned to see the PAPER SHEET, and written on it is a list of MOVIES AND PLAYS written in script. I'll give you a list when ya get to it. At the bottom of the list it also says: "I'm sure you'll enjoy them. CK" (*this stands for Carrie Kelley*)

MOVIE LIST:
on the waterfront
rebel without a cause
my left foot
cool hand luke
to kill a mockingbird
lawrence of arabia
the sand pebbles
grapes of wrath
the miracle worker
central station
gorillas in the mist
the lion in winter
china syndrome

Panel 6
Angle on Bruce as he closes the sketchbook while Titus watches.

Panel 7
Angle on Bruce standing beside the bed, his hand gently resting on the indentation on Damian's pillow.

PAGE 4

Panel 1
We're in the den, angle on Alfred's back, his hand holding up a thin canvas cover as he's looking at a PAINTING on an easel we can't see just yet.

Panel 2
Angle close on Alfred, trying to keep a stiff upper lip as he continues to hold the canvas cover up. Tears are streaming down his face as he stares at it.

Panel 3
Probably biggest on page. Angle only on the PAINTING Alfred's looking at. It matches the position all the Bat Family guys were in from issue #10 page 4. Make it more detailed, Pat, give the faces more weight and distinction than the original page. Anyway, the only difference is that DAMIAN IS UNFINISHED (a metaphor for his life). His body and face have been somewhat HALF COMPLETED, the rest of him is laid out/roughed in pencil. The other guys in the Bat Family are of course all finished.

Panel 4
Angle on Alfred with a hand over his eyes as he tries to control himself and hold back the tears.

Panel 5
Angle on Bruce in the shadows of the hallway watching Alfred and not wanting to step in and embarrass him. I'm guessing Alfred in foreground and Bruce in the background.

PAGE 5

Panel 1
Angle on Alfred knowing Bruce is approaching, as he pulls his jacket bottom straight with one hand and wipes his eyes with the back of his other hand without turning around. Think of that moment in Wrath of Khan when Spock is dying and he composes himself when he knows Kirk is there before turning around to face his old friend and captain.

Panel 2
Angle on Bruce as he joins Alfred at the painting staring at it together. Bruce has his hand on Alfred's shoulder.

Panel 3
Angle on Bruce as he starts to cover the painting, the last hint of Damian's unfinished figure staring back at us.

Panel 4
Angle on Alfred as he watches Bruce now slide the painting into a small inlaid wooden closet.

Panel 5
Angle on Alfred as he's turning the hands of a grandfather clock, which reveals the bat poles behind the bookcase that Bruce is stepping into. Look back at the way you showed the clock back in issue #1, page 6, panel 1. Alfred could be in the foreground and Bruce in the background.

PAGE 6

All vertical panels from top to bottom of page.

Panel 1
Vertical panel of Bruce sliding down the pole tunnel in the dim light (there are tiny LED lights running down the wall).

Panel 2
Angle on Bruce as he sees Damian sliding down the other pole right across from him, a smile (not goofy) on his face like he can't wait to suit up and hit the streets.

Panel 3
Angle from above of Bruce and Damian sliding down the poles in the darkness towards the light coming from the cave below.

Panel 4
Angle on Bruce as he's reached the bottom with no sign of Damian. All he sees is the pole and a thin trail of blood running down it.

Panel 5
Angle on Bruce as he reaches towards the pole but there's no blood now.

PAGE 7

Panel 1
Angle on Bruce at the lockers in his Bat suit without the cowl on. This is a bookend moment to the previous issue. Bruce is simply a warrior getting ready for his millionth battle as he puts on his gauntlets. He is standing there beside Damian's locker where we can see the Robin suit, gloves and boots ready to be worn.

Panel 2
Angle from behind Bruce as he stands in front of Damian's Robin uniform, simply staring at it.

Panel 3
Angle on Bruce as he places one of Damian's small Robin glove/gauntlets against the palm of his own large gloved hand. Think of it, Pat, like when your kid is born and you put that tiny little hand against yours and marvel at the difference in size.

Panel 4
Angle on Bruce as he's about to put his cowl on. His eyes have a lifelessness to them at this moment.

Panel 5
Angle on Batman walking past the case with Jason Todd's Robin suit. Angle this with the case in the foreground and Batman walking directly behind it without so much as giving it a glance. It's a profile shot so it appears in a way that Robin's uniform is superimposed over Batman.

Panel 6
Angle on Batman as he's now in the Batmobile, hitting a button on the console that starts to shut the canopy.

Panel 7
Thin horizontal, smallest on page as it barrels down the cave driveway.

PAGE 8

Splash (the one you already did).

Batman and Robin swinging through the Gotham cityscape.

Father and son on their nightly patrol.

Just a note: this page will need to be recolored so it reads as night and not dawn or dusk.

PAGE 9

Panel 1
Angle on Batman as he looks towards us over to Robin swinging beside him in the foreground, Robin's attention focused ahead, not aware his dad is looking at him. This is basically a closer shot of them in the splash except Bats is looking our way and he has a sense of subtle contentment across his face, proud to have his son with him, like all is right with the world.

Panel 2
Angle from Batman's perspective, behind his head, as we suddenly see that Robin is gone. There is no one swinging beside him all we see is an office building, lots of glass so we can see that only Batman is on patrol and also get a sense of the emptiness all around him in the reflection.

Panel 3
Angle closer on Batman's face as we now see that there's stubble on his face; his jaw tight as he realizes that Robin isn't there beside him.

Panel 4
Smallest on page. Close on a street sign that reads: PARK ROW. There are signs in NYC that are designed to have small squares on the sign that reveal some info about the street. This one should say: Gotham Historic District. Park Row. Would be great to have Batman's shadow seen moving across it.

Panel 5
Angle on Batman as he lands like a wraith on something we can't see just yet, his cape still up in the air behind him, the street sign we just saw visible in the background.

PAGE 10

Panel 1
Vertical panel. Half the page.

Batman crouching on top of the main pole of the old streetlight in Crime Alley that his parents were killed under. Angle this looking up at him so it feels more foreboding. PARK ROW/ CRIME ALLEY is still not a great neighborhood and I'm imagining that's it's taken somewhat of a beating in BATMAN INC. since I believe at the point that I'm writing this, Damian dies there. Now, whether that changes or not doesn't affect our scene except for the ref that will be needed on the current look of it. All that needs to be standing is the old streetlight where Bruce's parents and Damian died.

Think of this streetlight as the lone light in the darkness symbolically and figuratively.

Panel 2
Vertical panel. Half the page.

Reverse the camera angle so instead of looking up at Batman from the ground level, in this shot have the camera looking down at him atop the streetlight so we can see the halo of the light on the ground below.

PAGE 11

Panel 1
Angle close on Batman, grim, chin to chest, as he surveys the surroundings. He is all angst, sporting the look of someone wishing there was evil he could smash in the face.

Panel 2
Angle on Batman as he traces his fingers over the ornate ironwork at the top of the light.

Panel 3
Angle close on Batman as he pushes some small button on his utility belt or on his gauntlet. Your call, Pat, as to where you want to draw it.

Panel 4
Angle from just above Batman looking straight down so we see him, the streetlight and the cast-light over the Batmobile as it pulls in directly below, its canopy drawn back as he now leaps towards it.

PAGE 12

I'm seeing horizontal panels across for this page, Patrick.

Panel 1
Angle on Batman, gripping the wheel with two hands, as he drives off.

Panel 2
Angle on Batman as he turns to see Robin sitting in the passenger seat, focused on some controls on the console.

Panel 3
Angle from Batman's perspective as Robin is gone again and we can see in the side mirror the streetlight reflected back at us, a lone sentry of light on the street as he drives away.

Panel 4
Angle on Batman as he suddenly turns the wheel hard.

Panel 5
Angle straight on Batman through the windshield of the car as he comes racing towards us like a rocket, both hands gripped tightly on the wheel, determined.

Panel 6
Angle close on Batman's face; he's got that look of a man who doesn't care about anything at the moment.

PAGE 13

Panel 1
Biggest on page as the Batmobile smashes directly into the base of the streetlight, ripping it away like a tree from its roots, the electrical cables that were tied into the main cables underneath the street flapping and sparking as the Batmobile speeds through it.

Panel 2
Angle on the streetlight as it crashes to the pavement just behind the Batmobile.

Panel 3

Angle from behind the Batmobile as it continues speeding down the street towards the darkness, no light now whatsoever left in its wake.

PAGES 14 and 15

Double-page spread.

It's spooky Batman time. You don't want to face Batman on a regular crime-fighting night, right? Well, tonight is a night when his punches, kicks, and batarang throws are harder than ever.

What I'm thinking for this page, Pat, is something along the lines we did back in our Corps days. Instead of Yat/Arisia we instead have a dark figure of Batman holding up his arms and leaping at us in the center of the spread, and in the folds or shadows of his cape are several visceral images of Batman on the edge, all darkness and dread, more like the various bad guys are being attacked by Dracula/Nosferatu and they are scared @$%#&. Batman in these assorted images should be just a figure of darkness, more of a living shadow actually, just the whites of his eyes seen on occasion as he brings the pain to the scum of Gotham.

If ya want you can toss in one or two of our Batfreaks (not Shmush though), but also make sure these bad guys are vicious-looking fellas and in the middle of doing some evil #!&* as Bats takes them out.

Panel 1
Angle on GORDON asleep in his bed, no glasses, his cell phone ringing, the only light source.

Panel 2
Same angle on Gordon as he's still lying on his pillow only now he's got the cell pressed to his ear.

Panel 3
Angle from behind Gordon at his window, the curtain string in his hand, the curtain drawn up and the cell still pressed to his ear as we can see the BAT SIGNAL lit in the distance.

Panel 4
Angle close on Gordon's face, his glasses on, his hair slightly windswept as we're now atop police headquarters but we don't know it yet. Gordon's reaction is one of being taken aback by what he's seeing off panel.

Panel 5
Biggest on page. I'm thinking a high angle looking down at the Bat Signal shining bright in the darkness, Gordon is standing at the roof entrance beside BULLOCK and a UNIFORMED OFFICER as their gaze is fixed on the roof surface that is COVERED WITH BAD GUYS THAT BATMAN HAS "ARRESTED". The bad guys should be two or three deep stacked on top of each other, their hands and legs bound, with plastic tabs. Think of them like a deep-sea catch after the nets open up and flood the deck of a fishing boat.

PAGE 17

Panel 1
Thin horizontal. Smallest on page. Angle on the Batmobile as it pulls into the cave, Titus is there waiting expectantly, thinking somehow Damian is going to appear and get out of the car.

Panel 2
Angle on Titus following Batman, in full uniform, spattered with an extreme night of hard work which in his world of crime-fighting is blood, dirt and grim along with scratches and dents walks . He's not drenched in blood, but make sure we can read that it is indeed blood. Bats simply walks without any emotion, not acknowledging Titus.

Panel 3
I'd like to introduce a bit here that I thought would make sense in the details of Bruce's world, and that is we follow Batman as he walks through basically a small decontamination unit that sprays over his uniform, washing away the night of pain he delivered to the scum of Gotham; a baptism of sorts, a ritual that allows him to become Bruce Wayne again. Titus follows on the other side of the unit.

Panel 4
Angle on Batman as he's in the process of pulling off his cowl, other uniform pieces already placed into a specific "used" rack for Alfred to address later. The only thing Bruce should be wearing is an under-armor type of jumpsuit. We want him to be completely without his accoutrements, to show him vulnerable and human (but let's talk, maybe we should have him with his chest plate still on so we see the bat, I'm not sure). Anyway, we can see his row of other uniforms and utility belts, wirepoons, etc., in a hi-tech unit beside Damian's uniform unit. Titus continues to watch him and wait for some attention.

Panel 5
As Bruce starts to turn away from the lockers he slightly trips against Titus who still looks for Bruce to show him some love, affection, anything. You know that kinda moment when you're not paying attention when a dog is around and you stumble a bit. Have Bruce catch himself by grabbing hard at his locker, tilting it a bit, some stuff falling out, but specifically a FOLDED PIECE OF PAPER tucked into a small Bat device.

PAGE 18

Panel 1
Angle on Bruce as he still pays Titus no mind, as he picks up the fallen items from his locker.

Panel 2
Angle close on Bruce as he picks up the folded piece of paper.

Panel 3
Angle from behind Bruce as he reads the HANDWRITTEN NOTE.

NOTE: *I won't let you fight Leviathan alone. I need to help. But there's
something I have to tell you that I know I'll never be able to tell
you face to face, and that is my mother may have given me life,
but you taught me how to live, father.*

                        *Love and respect
your son,
Damian*

Panel 4
Angle from below looking up at Bruce reading the note, tears stream down his face.

Panel 5
Angle on Bruce as he leans back against the locker, his hands gripping the note tight.

PAGE 19

Panel 1
Angle on Bruce as he lets out a primal scream that only a parent can understand. It's the kind of scream we've never seen before from him -- uncontrolled, a roar of pain and loss.

Panels 2 thru 5
In these panels have Bruce literally smash apart everything in the locker area, lifting and throwing, punching and screaming, his hands getting bloody, pieces of his uniforms and Damian's in midair, scattered all over the place. All the while poor Titus watches.

Remember, Bruce should be in full tilt mode here, no holding back, all his emotions unchecked.

PAGE 20

Splash.

Looking down from above, but not too far up.

Bruce is on his knees, one hand clutching Damian's note, the other hand simply knuckles down, spent, chin to chest, shoulders and body slack, engulfed in the loss of his child.

Titus either stands there or is on his belly looking at Bruce, whatever you think looks best, Pat. A man and dog in pain.

Bat cowls and Robin cowls and uniforms, utility belts, gauntlets, boots, wirepoons, and other assorted stuff, etc, splayed and scattered around, visible.